AF442228

Table Of Contents

FOREWORD

I have many loves in my life. None are more important than my relationship with God. A close second is my wife and children. Fourth is my dog. Next to all of these is my love for the amazing, incredible nachos. Packed with such flavor in every bite, who cannot be head over heels for this tantalizing snack?

Their savoriness is second to none. I want to take a minute and thank my wife for cheerleading me through life and allowing me to be as weird as GOD made me to be. Love you with all my heart. I'm inclined to share some poems that I wrote about this snack.

POETRY: LAYERS OF FLAVOR: ODE TO NACHO

In the realm where cheese reigns supreme,
And salsa dances in a vibrant stream,
There lies a dish of crunchy delight,
Where every bite ignites the night.

Behold the nachos, a savory creation,
A symphony of flavors, a culinary sensation.

Upon a bed of golden chips, they lay,
Topped with ingredients in a colorful array.

Cheese cascades like a molten sun,
Melting hearts with each delicious run.

Beans, tomatoes, and jalapeños too,
A spicy chorus to tantalize and woo.

Guacamole, a creamy green oasis,
Adds a touch of freshness, a verdant basis.

Sour cream swirls, a cool contrast,
Balancing the heat with a gentle blast.

Oh, how these nachos, with their crispy crunch,
Elevate every gathering, every lunch.

They bring people together, in joyous cheer,
As we share this delectable frontier.

So let us raise a chip, with salsa adorned,
In celebration of nachos, forever adored.

In this simple dish, we find a treasure,
A symphony of taste that knows no measure.

POETRY: CHEESY SERENADE: A SONNET TO NACHOS

Of course! Here's a sonnet dedicated to the beloved nachos:

In golden hues, thy tortilla chips doth gleam,

Arrayed with toppings, a savory dream.

O' melted cheese, thy cloak of cheddar bold,

Enrobes each chip, a tale of taste untold.

From salsa's zest to beans of blackened hue,

And guacamole's creamy, verdant view,

Thy toppings dance in flavorful ballet,

A symphony of flavors in an array.

Oh, nachos dear, thy crunch so crisp and true,

Thy journey from the plate to mouth pursue.

With every bite, a burst of delight,

A fiesta in my mouth, oh what a sight!

So let us raise a chip unto the sky,

In praise of nachos, may they never die!

POETRY: LIVELY NACHOS: A LIMERICK FIESTA

There once was a plate piled with chips,
Topped with cheese and salsa in drips.

With each crispy crunch,
It's a savory lunch,

Oh, how nachos make taste buds do flips!

POETRY: CRISP DELIGHTS: A HAIKU TO NACHOS

Amidst crunchy chips,

Cheese and salsa dance in bliss,

Nachos delightfully.

CHAPTER 1

THE BIRTH OF A SNACK

In the vibrant town of Piedras Negras, Mexico, where the air was thick with the aroma of sizzling spices and the streets hummed with the lively chatter of locals and travelers alike, there lived a man whose culinary genius knew no bounds. Ignacio "Nacho" Anaya was his name, and he was a legend in his own right, revered for his unmatched skill in the kitchen and his unwavering dedication to the craft of cooking.

It was a sweltering summer day in the year 1943 when fate intervened and set the stage for Nacho's greatest culinary triumph. The Victory Club, a quaint little eatery tucked away on a bustling street corner, buzzed with activity as hungry patrons streamed through its doors, seeking respite from the scorching sun and the relentless heat.

Among the throng of customers was a group of weary U.S. military wives, their faces flushed with exhaustion and their stomachs growling with hunger. They had traveled far from home, seeking solace in the familiar comforts of American cuisine, only to find themselves in a foreign land with palates longing for a taste of home.

Nacho, ever the gracious host, greeted the women with a warm smile and a hearty welcome. But as he glanced over the menu, his heart sank. The offerings were decidedly Mexican – spicy enchiladas, sizzling fajitas, and hearty bowls of pozole – delicious, no doubt, but not quite what his American guests were craving.

It was in that moment of culinary crisis that inspiration struck like a bolt of lightning, igniting a spark of creativity within Nacho's soul. With a twinkle in his eye and a spring in his step, he darted into the kitchen, his mind racing with possibilities.

Rummaging through the pantry, Nacho gathered an assortment of ingredients – a bag of crispy tortilla chips, a block of creamy cheese, and a jar of fiery jalapeños. With the skill and precision of a seasoned chef, he set to work, his hands moving with the speed and grace of a conductor leading an orchestra.

Laying the chips out on a baking tray, Nacho piled them high with shredded cheese, watching with delight as it melted into a gooey, golden blanket of deliciousness. A few deft movements of the knife and the jalapeños were scattered on top, their vibrant green hue adding a pop of color to the dish.

With a flourish, Nacho slid the tray into the oven, the heat of the flames enveloping the chips and cheese in a warm embrace. As he watched through the oven window, a sense of anticipation washed over him, mingling with the heady aroma of melted cheese and spicy peppers that filled the air.

Minutes ticked by like hours as Nacho waited with bated breath, his heart pounding in his chest. And then, finally, it was time. With a triumphant grin, he pulled the tray from the oven, the nachos sizzling and bubbling with
irresistible allure.

With a flourish, he presented the dish to his guests, their eyes widening in disbelief at the sight before them. Nacho's nachos, as they would soon come to be known, were a revelation – a symphony of flavors and textures that danced across the palate with every bite.

And just like that, a legend was born. Ignacio "Nacho" Anaya had unwittingly stumbled upon something truly extraordinary – a snack that would capture the hearts (and stomachs) of people around the world, one crunchy chip at a time.

Little did Nacho know that his simple creation would spark a nacho revolution, forever cementing his place in culinary history as the father of nachos. But for now, as he watched his guests devouring the cheesy delights before them, all he could do was smile, knowing that he had created something truly magical.

CHAPTER 2

A CRUNCHY REVOLUTION

The nacho revolution was in full swing, and Nacho Anaya was at the helm, steering the course of culinary history with his boundless enthusiasm and unwavering dedication to all things cheesy and delicious. But as the popularity of nachos soared to new heights, so too did the creativity of those who sought to put their unique spin on the classic snack.

From the bustling streets of New York City to the sun-drenched beaches of California, nacho fever swept the nation, leaving a trail of cheesy goodness in its wake. Restaurants and food trucks vied for the title of "ultimate nacho destination," each offering up their tantalizing variations on the beloved dish.

But it wasn't just about the nachos themselves – it was about the experience. Nacho-themed events and festivals popped up in cities across the country, drawing crowds of eager foodies and nacho enthusiasts eager to celebrate their favorite snack in all its crunchy glory.

At these events, chefs and home cooks alike showcased their creativity, dreaming up wild and waScky nacho creations that pushed the boundaries of culinary imagination. From loaded nacho fries to nacho-topped pizzas, there seemed to be no limit to the delicious ways you could enjoy this beloved snack.

But perhaps the most exciting development of all was the rise of the DIY nacho bar. Inspired by the communal spirit of Mexican street food culture, these interactive stations allowed diners to customize their nachos to their heart's content, piling on their favorite toppings with reckless abandon.

And as the nacho craze continued to sweep the nation, it wasn't long before Hollywood took notice. Nachos began popping up in movies and TV shows, cementing their status as a cultural icon beloved by people of all ages and backgrounds.

But through it all, Nacho Anaya remained the undisputed king of nachos, his name synonymous with cheesy goodness and culinary innovation. Though he may have passed on to the great kitchen in the sky, his legacy lived on in every crunchy bite of nacho goodness.

As we look back on the nacho revolution with fondness and nostalgia, let us raise a crunchy chip in honor of Nacho Anaya – the visionary chef who dared to dream of a world where nachos reigned supreme.

CHAPTER 3

NACHO MANIA

As the nacho revolution continued its relentless march across the culinary landscape, a tidal wave of nacho mania swept over the nation like a cheesy tsunami, leaving a trail of crunchy satisfaction in its wake. From the bustling streets of New York City to the sun-drenched beaches of California, everyone seemed to be caught up in the nacho frenzy, eagerly embracing the cheesy goodness that had captured the nation's imagination.

Nacho-themed parties weren't just a passing trend – they were a way of life. Hosts went to extravagant lengths to transform their homes into nacho wonderlands, adorning every surface with cheesy decorations and whimsical nacho-themed props. Guests arrived dressed as giant tortilla chips, their faces painted with colorful nacho toppings, ready to indulge in a night of cheesy revelry.

But it wasn't just about the parties – it was about the experience. Nacho enthusiasts flocked to themed events and festivals, eager to sample the latest and greatest in nacho innovation. From gourmet nacho tastings to nacho cook-offs judged by celebrity chefs, there was no shortage of ways to celebrate everyone's favorite snack.

And with the rise of social media, nachos became more than just a food – they became a lifestyle. Instagram feeds were flooded with photos of towering nacho mountains and gooey cheese pulls, each more drool-worthy than the last. Hashtags like #nachogoals and #cheesygoodness trended worldwide, as people shared their love for nachos with the click of a button.

But perhaps the most heartwarming aspect of nacho mania was its ability to bring people together. Whether gathered around a table at a neighborhood taqueria or huddled together on the couch for a movie night at home, nachos had a way of breaking down barriers and fostering a sense of community. Families bonded over shared trays of nachos, while friends laughed and reminisced over plates piled high with cheesy goodness.

And as the nacho craze continued to spread, it wasn't long before enterprising entrepreneurs began capitalizing on the trend. Nacho-themed merchandise flooded the market, from t-shirts and hats to keychains and tote bags, each proudly proclaiming the wearer's love for all things cheesy. Restaurants and food trucks cashed in on the craze, offering up wild and wacky nacho creations that pushed the boundaries of culinary imagination.

But through it all, Nacho Anaya remained the guiding light of the nacho movement, his legacy living on in every crunchy chip and gooey cheese pull. Though he may have passed on to the great kitchen in the sky, his spirit lived on in the hearts of nacho lovers everywhere, inspiring them to dream big and eat even bigger.

And so, as we look back on the golden age of nacho mania with fondness and nostalgia, let us raise a crunchy chip in honor of Nacho Anaya – the visionary chef who dared to dream of a world where nachos reigned supreme.

CHAPTER 4

NACHO LEGENDS

As the nacho revolution continued its unstoppable march, Nacho Anaya's humble creation transcended its origins to become a cultural icon, revered by people from all walks of life. But Nacho's impact stretched far beyond the confines of his beloved Piedras Negras – he was a culinary pioneer, a visionary whose ingenuity and passion for food would forever alter the snacking landscape.

In the years following his groundbreaking creation at the Victory Club, Nacho's legend grew, his name whispered in reverent tones by grateful patrons and aspiring chefs alike. His innovative spirit and boundless creativity had transformed a simple dish into a culinary phenomenon that would capture the hearts (and stomachs) of people around the world.

But Nacho was more than just a talented chef – he was a trailblazer, a maverick in the kitchen who dared to defy convention and forge his path. His invention of the nacho may have been born out of necessity, but it was his unwavering dedication to his craft that propelled it to greatness.

As nachos continued to evolve, so too did Nacho himself. He dedicated his life to perfecting his craft and sharing his love for nachos with anyone who would listen. From humble beginnings at the Victory Club to international acclaim, Nacho's journey was a testament to the power of passion and perseverance.

But Nacho's influence extended far beyond the borders of Piedras Negras. His simple yet inspired creation inspired a new generation of chefs and food enthusiasts, each eager to put their unique spin on the classic snack.

Restaurants and food trucks began offering up wild and wacky nacho creations that pushed the boundaries of culinary imagination. From loaded nacho fries to nacho-topped pizzas, there seemed to be no limit to the delicious ways you could enjoy this beloved dish.

But perhaps the most exciting development of all was the rise of gourmet nacho joints, where chefs treated nachos with the same reverence and respect as fine dining cuisine. These culinary wizards experimented with exotic ingredients and intricate flavor combinations, elevating nachos from a humble snack to a gourmet delicacy.

And as the years passed, nachos continued to evolve, adapting to the ever-changing tastes and trends of the culinary world. But through it all, one thing remained constant – the spirit of innovation and creativity that Nacho Anaya had instilled in the snack so many years ago.

Today, Nacho's legacy lives on in every crunchy chip and gooey cheese pull. Though he may have passed on to the great kitchen in the sky, his spirit lives on in the hearts of nacho lovers everywhere, inspiring them to dream big and eat even bigger.

And so, as we look back on the legacy of Nacho Anaya and the evolution of nachos, let us raise a crunchy chip in his honor – the visionary chef who dared to dream of a world where nachos reigned supreme

CHAPTER 5

THE FUTURE OF NACHOS

As we peer into the tantalizing abyss of the future, one thing becomes abundantly clear – nachos are not just a passing trend but a timeless culinary delight that will continue to evolve and captivate generations to come. With each passing year, new innovations and culinary experiments push the boundaries of what nachos can be, tantalizing taste buds and igniting imaginations around the globe.

But what does the future hold for our beloved snack? Will nachos continue to evolve and adapt to the ever-changing culinary landscape, or will they remain steadfast in their traditional form, a comforting reminder of simpler times?

One thing is for certain – the possibilities are as endless as the cheesy goodness of nachos themselves. With advancements in technology and a growing interest in sustainable and plant-based foods, the future of nachos is brighter than ever before.

Imagine a world where nacho toppings are sourced from vertical farms, utilizing cutting-edge hydroponic and aeroponic techniques to grow fresh produce year-round. Picture a nacho chip crafted from ancient grains or nutrient-rich vegetables, offering a healthier alternative without sacrificing flavor or crunch.

But it's not just about the ingredients – it's about the experience. In the future, nacho bars may become interactive hubs of culinary creativity, where diners can customize their nachos with a dizzying array of toppings and sauces, from traditional favorites to exotic flavors from around the world.

And as technology continues to advance, who's to say what other innovations lie in store for nachos? Augmented reality overlays could enhance the dining experience, allowing patrons to visualize their nachos in exciting new ways before they even take a bite. Meanwhile, 3D printing technology could revolutionize the way nachos are crafted, allowing for intricate designs and shapes that were once thought impossible.

But perhaps the most exciting aspect of the future of nachos is its ability to bring people together. In a world that often feels divided, nachos have a way of breaking down barriers and fostering a sense of community. Whether shared with friends at a backyard barbecue or enjoyed solo on a cozy night in, nachos have a way of bringing joy and laughter to all who partake.

So as we gaze into the crystal ball of culinary innovation, let us raise a crunchy chip in anticipation of the delicious delights that await us. Whether you prefer your nachos piled high with all the fixings or keep it simple with just cheese and jalapeños, one thing is for certain – the future of nachos is looking brighter than ever before.

And so, as we embark on this cheesy adventure together, let us savor every crunchy bite and relish in the delicious possibilities that lie ahead. The future of nachos is limitless, and we can't wait to see where it takes us.

NACHOS
AROUND
WORLD

MEXICO
City

1.) MEXICO CITY, MEXICO

Mexico City, the sprawling capital of Mexico, is not only a cultural hub but also the birthplace of nachos. Here, you can embark on a culinary journey through the streets, markets, and restaurants, discovering the diverse array of nacho offerings that reflect the rich tapestry of Mexican cuisine.

Begin your nacho adventure at one of the city's bustling street food stalls, where vendors skillfully assemble simple yet satisfying plates of nachos. Freshly fried tortilla chips, made from locally sourced corn, form the base of these iconic snacks. The chips are then generously smothered in melted cheese—often a blend of Oaxaca and Chihuahua cheese—creating a gooey, indulgent layer that binds the toppings together. But the true beauty of nachos lies in their versatility, and Mexico City's culinary scene showcases this with an array of topping options. Traditionalists might opt for classic toppings such as refried beans, diced tomatoes, sliced jalapeños, and tangy salsa verde or roja. Meanwhile, adventurous eaters can sample innovative twists on the classic dish, featuring ingredients like tender cochinita pibil, savory barbacoa, or creamy guacamole made from ripe avocados sourced from nearby orchards.

As you explore the city's neighborhoods, you'll encounter restaurants and cantinas that elevate nachos to gourmet heights. From sleek modern eateries to rustic taquerías, each establishment puts its own spin on the beloved dish, incorporating regional flavors and culinary techniques. Indulge in nachos topped with succulent grilled meats, tangy pickled onions, and crumbled queso fresco, or savor the richness of mole poblano drizzled over a mound of crispy chips.

No visit to Mexico City would be complete without sampling the city's vibrant street food culture, where nachos are just one of many tantalizing offerings. Wander through the bustling stalls of Mercado de San Juan or Mercado de la Merced, where the air is thick with the aroma of spices and sizzling meats. Take a seat at a plastic table adorned with vibrant papel picado and enjoy a plate of nachos while soaking in the sights and sounds of this culinary wonderland.

In Mexico City, nachos are more than just a snack—they're a celebration of culture, tradition, and the joy of good food shared with loved ones. Whether you're indulging in street food delights or dining at a Michelin-starred restaurant, you'll find that each bite of nachos tells a story, reflecting the rich history and culinary heritage of this dynamic city.

LOVE
THE
AUSTIN
WAY

2.) AUSTIN, TEXAS, USA

Austin, the capital of Texas, is a city renowned for its vibrant music scene, eclectic culture, and, of course, its mouthwatering cuisine. When it comes to nachos, Austin takes the dish to new heights, offering a plethora of options that cater to every palate and preference.

Start your nacho adventure in the heart of downtown Austin, where food trucks line the streets, offering creative takes on the classic Tex-Mex dish. Step up to the window of a brightly colored truck adorned with graffiti-style murals and place your order for loaded nachos piled high with brisket smoked to perfection. Watch as the vendor expertly layers on melted cheese, tangy BBQ sauce, and crunchy pickled jalapeños, creating a symphony of flavors and textures that dance across your taste buds.

But Austin's nacho scene extends far beyond the confines of food trucks, with restaurants and bars throughout the city putting their unique spin on the beloved dish. Head to a cozy neighborhood joint where locals gather to watch the game and indulge in plates of nachos topped with queso blanco, black beans, and spicy chorizo. Or, for a more upscale experience, dine at a trendy gastropub where nachos are elevated to gourmet status, featuring artisanal cheeses, house-made salsas, and decadent toppings like truffle oil and avocado crema.

As you explore Austin's culinary landscape, you'll discover that the city's nacho offerings are as diverse as its music venues. From traditional Tex-Mex eateries serving up hearty plates of nachos smothered in chili con carne to hipster cafes offering vegan-friendly options made with plant-based cheese and fresh, locally sourced ingredients, there's something for everyone to enjoy.

No visit to Austin would be complete without sampling the city's famous breakfast tacos, a beloved morning staple that pairs perfectly with a side of nachos. Head to a bustling taco joint in the heart of the city and order a breakfast taco filled with scrambled eggs, crispy bacon, and creamy avocado, accompanied by a side of nachos topped with pico de gallo and tangy queso dip.

In Austin, nachos aren't just a dish—they're a way of life. Whether you're sampling street food delights from a food truck or dining at a chic restaurant overlooking Lady Bird Lake, you'll find that each bite of nachos tells a story, reflecting the unique spirit and flavor of this dynamic city.

LOS
ANGELES
CALIFORNIA REPUBLIC

3.) LOS ANGELES, CALIFORNIA, USA

Los Angeles, the sprawling metropolis nestled between mountains and ocean, is a melting pot of cultures, cuisines, and culinary creativity. When it comes to nachos, this vibrant city offers a dizzying array of options that span the spectrum from classic comfort food to innovative fusion fare.

Embark on your nacho journey amidst the vibrant hustle of Downtown LA, where historical landmarks blend seamlessly with modern skyscrapers and food trucks beckon with mouthwatering offerings. Approach a vividly painted truck adorned with neon lights and place your order for a heaping plate of nachos piled high with all the trimmings—oozing cheese, zesty salsa, velvety guacamole, and a lavish dollop of tangy sour cream. Find a nearby bench to perch on and relish your feast while immersing yourself in the lively ambiance of the bustling cityscape.

However, the true allure of nachos lies in their adaptability, and Los Angeles capitalizes on this, presenting a diverse array of nacho variations to cater to every palate and dietary preference. Venture to a trendy gastropub in Silver Lake, where you can indulge in artisanal nachos crafted from locally procured ingredients and inventive toppings such as kimchi, succulent pork belly, and fiery sriracha aioli. Alternatively, for a taste of timeless Hollywood glamour, dine at a storied eatery along the iconic Sunset Strip, where you can relish a platter of nachos alongside a meticulously crafted cocktail and panoramic vistas of the city skyline.

As you traverse the eclectic neighborhoods of Los Angeles, you'll encounter dining establishments that draw inspiration from culinary traditions spanning the globe, resulting in nacho creations as diverse and eclectic as the city itself. From Korean-infused nachos adorned with savory bulgogi beef and spicy gochujang sauce to Mexican-Korean fusion tacos accompanied by a side of kimchi-infused nachos, the culinary landscape of the City of Angels offers a kaleidoscope of gastronomic delights awaiting exploration.

No visit to Los Angeles would be complete without sampling the city's famous street food scene, where you can find some of the best nachos in town from vendors who have perfected the art of crafting delicious, portable meals on the go. Whether you're strolling along Venice Beach, browsing the boutiques of Melrose Avenue, or exploring the historic landmarks of Olvera Street, you're sure to encounter a tempting array of nacho options that will satisfy your cravings and leave

San Antonio

4.). SAN ANTONIO, TEXAS, USA

Nestled in the heart of the Lone Star State, San Antonio stands as a beacon of Tex-Mex cuisine, drawing food enthusiasts from far and wide to indulge in its rich culinary offerings. Renowned for its vibrant flavors and hearty portions, San Antonio's nacho scene is a testament to the city's love affair with all things spicy, cheesy, and utterly satisfying.

Begin your exploration of San Antonio's nacho culture along the iconic River Walk, where picturesque waterways wind through the city center, flanked by charming restaurants and lively bars. Take a seat at a waterfront eatery and prepare to be transported to nacho paradise as you peruse menus brimming with mouthwatering options. From classic renditions featuring smoky refried beans and zesty pico de gallo to innovative creations boasting tangy BBQ brisket and creamy queso fresco, the possibilities are as endless as the river's gentle flow.

Venture beyond the tourist-laden paths of the River Walk to uncover hidden gems scattered throughout San Antonio's diverse neighborhoods. In the historic district of Market Square, known locally as El Mercado, you'll find bustling plazas lined with colorful stalls and traditional taquerías serving up authentic Tex-Mex fare. Pull up a chair beneath a canopy of papel picado and treat yourself to a plate of nachos piled high with tender carne asada, velvety avocado slices, and a fiery salsa roja that packs a punch.

For a taste of San Antonio's modern culinary scene, head to the city's trendy Southtown district, where hip gastropubs and fusion eateries put their spin on the classic nacho dish. Indulge in gourmet nachos featuring locally sourced ingredients like juicy chorizo sausage, roasted poblano peppers, and crumbled queso fresco, all expertly crafted into a symphony of flavor that will tantalize your taste buds and leave you craving more.

In San Antonio, nachos aren't just a dish—they're a way of life, woven into the fabric of the city's culture and cherished by locals and visitors alike. So come hungry, bring your appetite, and prepare to embark on a nacho-fueled adventure through the heart of Texas, where every bite tells a story of flavor, tradition, and the unbridled joy of good food shared with good company.

New York

5.) NEW YORK CITY, NEW YORK, USA

In the bustling metropolis of New York City, where the streets pulse with energy and the skyline stretches towards the heavens, one culinary delight stands out among the rest: nachos. From the trendy eateries of Manhattan to the hidden gems of Brooklyn and beyond, New York City offers a diverse array of nacho experiences that are as unique and vibrant as the city itself.

Start your nacho odyssey in the heart of Manhattan, where world-class chefs and innovative restaurateurs push the boundaries of flavor and creativity to deliver unforgettable nacho experiences. Step into a sleek gastropub in the East Village and treat yourself to a plate of gourmet nachos piled high with succulent braised short rib, tangy pickled onions, and a drizzle of smoky chipotle aioli, all served atop a bed of crisp tortilla chips that crunch with every bite.

For a taste of old-school New York charm, venture to one of the city's legendary dive bars, where time-worn jukeboxes and neon signs beckon patrons to unwind with a cold beer and a plate of classic nachos. Dive into a mountain of cheesy goodness, adorned with velvety melted cheese, chunky salsa, and creamy sour cream, all served with a side of lively conversation and the comforting hum of the city outside.

But the true beauty of nachos in New York City lies in their ability to reflect the city's melting pot of cultures and culinary influences. Explore the vibrant neighborhoods of Queens, where authentic Mexican taquerías dish up traditional nachos bursting with flavor and spice. Or head to the Bronx, where Caribbean eateries infuse their nachos with tropical flair, adding juicy pineapple salsa and tangy jerk chicken to the mix for a taste of island paradise.

No matter where your nacho journey takes you in New York City, one thing is certain: you're in for a culinary adventure like no other. So grab a fork, grab a friend, and get ready to explore the bold and flavorful world of nachos in the city that never sleeps.

Toronto

6.) TORONTO, CANADA

Nestled on the shores of Lake Ontario, the multicultural metropolis of Toronto beckons visitors with its vibrant neighborhoods, diverse culinary scene, and tantalizing array of nacho offerings. From bustling street markets to cozy neighborhood joints, Toronto offers a melting pot of flavors and influences that come together to create nachos that are as delicious as they are diverse.

Begin your nacho expedition in the heart of downtown Toronto, where trendy gastropubs and chic eateries serve up gourmet takes on the classic dish. Sink your teeth into a plate of artisanal nachos featuring locally sourced ingredients like tender braised pork, tangy pickled jalapeños, and creamy avocado salsa, all served atop a bed of crispy tortilla chips that crackle with each bite.

For a taste of Toronto's vibrant street food scene, head to the bustling markets of Kensington Market, where vendors dish up authentic nachos bursting with flavor and spice. Wander through the narrow alleys and colorful stalls, sampling plates of nachos piled high with savory meats, tangy cheeses, and fiery salsas that transport your taste buds to the bustling markets of Mexico.

But Toronto's nacho scene isn't confined to its downtown core—venture into the city's diverse neighborhoods to discover hidden gems that cater to every taste and dietary preference. From vegan-friendly nachos made with plant-based cheese and fresh vegetables to halal options featuring tender halal meats and aromatic spices, there's something for everyone to enjoy in this multicultural metropolis.

No visit to Toronto would be complete without sampling the city's famous craft beer scene, which pairs perfectly with a plate of loaded nachos. Whether you're sipping on a hoppy IPA or a rich stout, the bold flavors of Toronto's craft brews complement the spicy and savory notes of its beloved nachos, creating a culinary experience that's as satisfying as it is memorable.

In Toronto, nachos are more than just a dish—they're a celebration of flavor, culture, and the vibrant spirit of Canada's largest city. So come hungry, come thirsty, and prepare to embark on a nacho-fueled journey through the heart of Toronto, where every bite is a delicious adventure waiting to be savored.

TOKYO

7.) TOKYO, JAPAN

Tokyo, the bustling capital of Japan, stands as a vibrant hub of culinary innovation, where traditional Japanese flavors blend harmoniously with international influences to create a diverse and exciting food scene. While not traditionally associated with nachos, Tokyo surprises visitors with its unique interpretations of this Tex-Mex classic, offering a fusion of flavors that tantalize the taste buds and reflect the city's creative spirit.

Step into one of Tokyo's trendy izakayas, traditional Japanese taverns with a modern twist, and prepare to embark on a culinary adventure like no other. Here, chefs draw inspiration from both local and global ingredients to craft innovative nacho creations that marry the bold flavors of Tex-Mex cuisine with the delicate nuances of Japanese cooking.

Indulge in nachos topped with succulent slices of Wagyu beef, marinated in soy sauce and mirin for a hint of sweetness, then grilled to perfection. Crisp nori flakes add a touch of umami richness, while creamy avocado and tangy yuzu salsa provide a refreshing contrast. Each bite is a symphony of flavors that dance across your palate, showcasing the culinary ingenuity of Tokyo's chefs.

Tokyo's nacho scene isn't confined to its upscale izakayas—venture into the city's vibrant street food markets to discover hidden gems that cater to adventurous eaters in search of bold and exciting flavors. Here, food stalls offer inventive twists on the classic nacho dish, from tempura-battered tortilla chips drizzled with wasabi mayo to nachos topped with crispy fried tofu and spicy kimchi, creating a fusion of flavors that reflects Tokyo's multicultural landscape.

No visit to Tokyo would be complete without sampling the city's famous ramen shops, where steaming bowls of noodles simmer in rich, flavorful broths. Pair your ramen with a side of nachos featuring tender slices of chashu pork, savory miso cheese sauce, and crunchy bamboo shoots for a satisfying meal that blends the best of Tex-Mex and Japanese cuisine.

In Tokyo, nachos transcend their culinary origins—they symbolize a tribute to creative culinary expression and the lively essence of fusion cuisine. So, whether you arrive famished or simply intrigued, get ready to embark on a nacho-infused expedition through Tokyo's bustling streets, where each mouthful promises a delightful fusion of flavors and experiences.

Sydney

8.) SYDNEY, AUSTRALIA

Sydney, the sun-kissed capital of New South Wales, is a city of stunning beaches, iconic landmarks, and a thriving culinary scene that reflects its multicultural population and diverse influences. While not traditionally associated with nachos, Sydney surprises visitors with its unique interpretations of this Tex-Mex classic, offering a fusion of flavors that celebrate the city's laid-back coastal lifestyle.

Head to Bondi Beach, one of Sydney's most famous destinations, and prepare to indulge in nachos with a view. Take a seat at a beachside café overlooking the sparkling waters of the Pacific Ocean and order a plate of loaded nachos featuring fresh, locally sourced ingredients. Savor the flavors of the sea with nachos topped with succulent prawns, creamy avocado, and tangy lime salsa, all served atop a bed of crispy tortilla chips that capture the essence of coastal living.

Yet Sydney's nacho scene isn't limited to its shoreline—explore the city's lively districts to uncover hidden culinary gems tailored to food enthusiasts seeking bold and adventurous flavors. From stylish rooftop bars in Surry Hills to quaint cafes in Newtown, Sydney offers a plethora of options for nacho aficionados eager to indulge in this beloved Tex-Mex delight.

A visit to Sydney wouldn't be fully experienced without indulging in the city's renowned seafood, ideally paired with a generous serving of loaded nachos. Whether you're savoring freshly shucked oysters with a side of salsa verde or treating yourself to crispy battered haddock drizzled with spicy chipotle aioli, Sydney's vibrant seafood flavors harmonize flawlessly with the savory and spicy profiles of its cherished nachos, resulting in a culinary journey that's both memorable and mouthwatering.

In Sydney, nachos represent more than just a dish—they embody a celebration of flavor, culture, and the lively essence of Australia's most iconic city.

London
TELEPHONE

9.) LONDON, ENGLAND

London, the historic and cosmopolitan capital of England, is a city renowned for its rich history, cultural diversity, and thriving food scene. While not traditionally associated with nachos, London surprises visitors with its eclectic culinary offerings, offering unique interpretations of this Tex-Mex classic that reflect the city's multicultural influences and innovative spirit.

Enter one of London's trendy gastropubs, where traditional British fare meets international flavors, and prepare to indulge in nachos with a twist. Here, chefs draw inspiration from cuisines around the world to create innovative nacho creations that push the boundaries of flavor and creativity.

Indulge in nachos featuring tender lamb shawarma, creamy tzatziki, and zesty harissa sauce, all served atop a bed of crispy tortilla chips that capture the essence of Middle Eastern cuisine. Or opt for nachos topped with fragrant Indian spices, tangy mango chutney, and cooling raita, creating a dish that's as comforting as it is flavorful.

But London's nacho scene isn't confined to its gastropubs—venture into the city's vibrant neighborhoods to discover hidden gems that cater to food enthusiasts in search of bold and exciting flavors. From bustling street markets in Camden to cozy cafes in Shoreditch, London offers a myriad of options for nacho lovers looking to indulge in this beloved Tex-Mex treat.

Coming to London wouldn't be complete without sampling the city's famous fish and chips, which pair perfectly with a plate of loaded nachos. Whether you're enjoying flaky cod with a side of salsa verde or indulging in crispy battered haddock drizzled with spicy chipotle aioli, the bold flavors of London's seafood scene complement the savory and spicy notes of its beloved nachos, creating a culinary experience that's as unforgettable as it is delicious.

BARCELONA
.1899

10.) BARCELONA, SPAIN

Barcelona, the cosmopolitan capital of Catalonia, is renowned for its stunning architecture, vibrant street life, and thriving food scene. While not traditionally associated with nachos, Barcelona surprises visitors with its eclectic culinary offerings, offering unique interpretations of this Tex-Mex classic that reflect the city's multicultural influences and creative spirit.

Enter one of Barcelona's trendy tapas bars, where traditional Spanish fare meets international flavors, and prepare to indulge in nachos with a twist. Here, chefs draw inspiration from cuisines around the world to create innovative nacho creations that push the boundaries of flavor and creativity.

Indulge in nachos featuring tender chorizo, creamy manchego cheese, and smoky paprika sauce, all served atop a bed of crispy tortilla chips that capture the essence of Spanish cuisine. Or opt for nachos topped with fragrant Moroccan spices, tangy preserved lemon, and cooling yogurt sauce, creating a dish that's as comforting as it is flavorful.

A trip to Barcelona isn't complete without trying the city's famous paella, ideally accompanied by a plate of loaded nachos. Whether you're opting for a traditional seafood paella with a side of salsa verde or indulging in a robust meat and vegetable paella topped with spicy chipotle aioli, the rich flavors of Barcelona's cuisine perfectly complement the savory and spicy elements of its beloved nachos, resulting in a culinary experience that's both unforgettable and delectable.

In Barcelona, nachos aren't just a dish—they're a celebration of flavor, culture, and the vibrant atmosphere of one of Europe's most iconic cities. So, whether you're arriving with a hearty appetite or a sense of curiosity, prepare to embark on a nacho-centric journey through Barcelona's bustling streets, where each bite promises an adventure in taste and tradition.

RECIPE
FOR
NACHOS

RECIPE: THE ORIGINAL

Ingredients :

- Tortilla chips
- 1 cup shredded cheese (cheddar, Monterey Jack, or a blend)
- 1/2 cup black beans, drained and rinsed
- 1/4 cup diced tomatoes
- 1/4 cup diced red onion
- 1/4 cup sliced black olives
- 1/4 cup sliced jalapeños (optional, for added spice)
- 1/4 cup chopped fresh cilantro
- 1 avocado, diced
- Sour cream, for serving
- Salsa, for serving

Instructions :

- Preheat your oven to 350°F (175°C).
- Arrange a layer of tortilla chips on a baking sheet or oven-safe dish in a single layer.
- Sprinkle half of the shredded cheese evenly over the tortilla chips.
- Spread the black beans, diced tomatoes, red onion, black olives, and jalapeños (if using) evenly over the cheese.

- Sprinkle the remaining shredded cheese over the top of the nachos.

- Place the baking sheet or dish in the preheated oven and bake for about 10-12 minutes, or until the cheese is melted and bubbly.

- Remove the nachos from the oven and let them cool for a minute or two.

- Top the nachos with diced avocado and chopped cilantro.

- Serve the nachos with sour cream and salsa on the side for dipping.

- Enjoy your delicious homemade nachos! Feel free to customize them with additional toppings like cooked ground beef or shredded chicken if desired.

Recipe: Korean BBQ Pork Belly Nachos

Ingredients:

- 1 lb pork belly, thinly sliced
- 1 cup Korean BBQ sauce (store-bought or homemade)
- 1 bag (10-12 oz) tortilla chips
- 1 cup shredded mozzarella cheese
- 1 cup shredded Monterey Jack cheese
- 1/2 cup kimchi, chopped
- 1/4 cup green onions, thinly sliced
- 1/4 cup cilantro, chopped
- 1/4 cup sour cream
- 1/4 cup gochujang (Korean chili paste)
- 1 tablespoon sesame seeds
- 1 tablespoon vegetable oil
- Salt and pepper to taste

Instructions :

- Preheat your oven to 400°F (200°C).
- In a skillet over medium heat, add vegetable oil. Season the pork belly slices with salt and pepper, then add them to the skillet. Cook until the pork belly is crispy and caramelized, about 3-4 minutes per side.

- Once the pork belly is cooked, remove it from the skillet and chop it into bite-sized pieces. Return the pork belly to the skillet and add Korean BBQ sauce. Stir to coat the pork belly pieces in the sauce, then simmer for 2-3 minutes until the sauce thickens slightly.

- Spread a layer of tortilla chips on a baking sheet or oven-safe dish.

- Sprinkle shredded mozzarella and Monterey Jack cheese over the tortilla chips.

- Top the cheese with the Korean BBQ pork belly mixture.

- Add chopped kimchi on top of the pork belly.

- Bake in the preheated oven for about 5-7 minutes, or until the cheese is melted and bubbly.

- Remove from the oven and sprinkle with sliced green onions, chopped cilantro, and sesame seeds.

- Drizzle sour cream and gochujang over the top of the nachos.

- Serve immediately and enjoy your unique Korean BBQ Pork Belly Nach

Recipe: Texas BBQ Brisket Nachos

Ingredients:

- Tortilla chips
- 1 lb Texas-style BBQ brisket, cooked and shredded
- 1 cup shredded cheddar cheese
- 1 cup shredded Monterey Jack cheese
- 1/2 cup diced red onion
- 1/2 cup diced pickled jalapeños
- 1/4 cup chopped fresh cilantro
- 1/4 cup BBQ sauce (Texas-style, if available)
- 1/4 cup sour cream
- 1/4 cup guacamole
- Sliced green onions for garnish

Instructions:

- Preheat your oven to 350°F (175°C).
- Arrange a layer of tortilla chips on a baking sheet or oven-safe dish.
- Spread the cooked and shredded Texas-style BBQ brisket evenly over the chips.

- Sprinkle shredded cheddar and Monterey Jack cheese over the brisket.

- Scatter diced red onion and diced pickled jalapeños over the cheese.

- Drizzle BBQ sauce over the nachos.

- Bake in the preheated oven for about 10-15 minutes, or until the cheese is melted and bubbly.

- Remove from the oven and garnish with chopped fresh cilantro and sliced green onions.

- Serve hot with dollops of sour cream and guacamole on top.

- Enjoy your Texas BBQ Brisket Nachos with a true taste of Texas flavor!

Notes for your Recipes

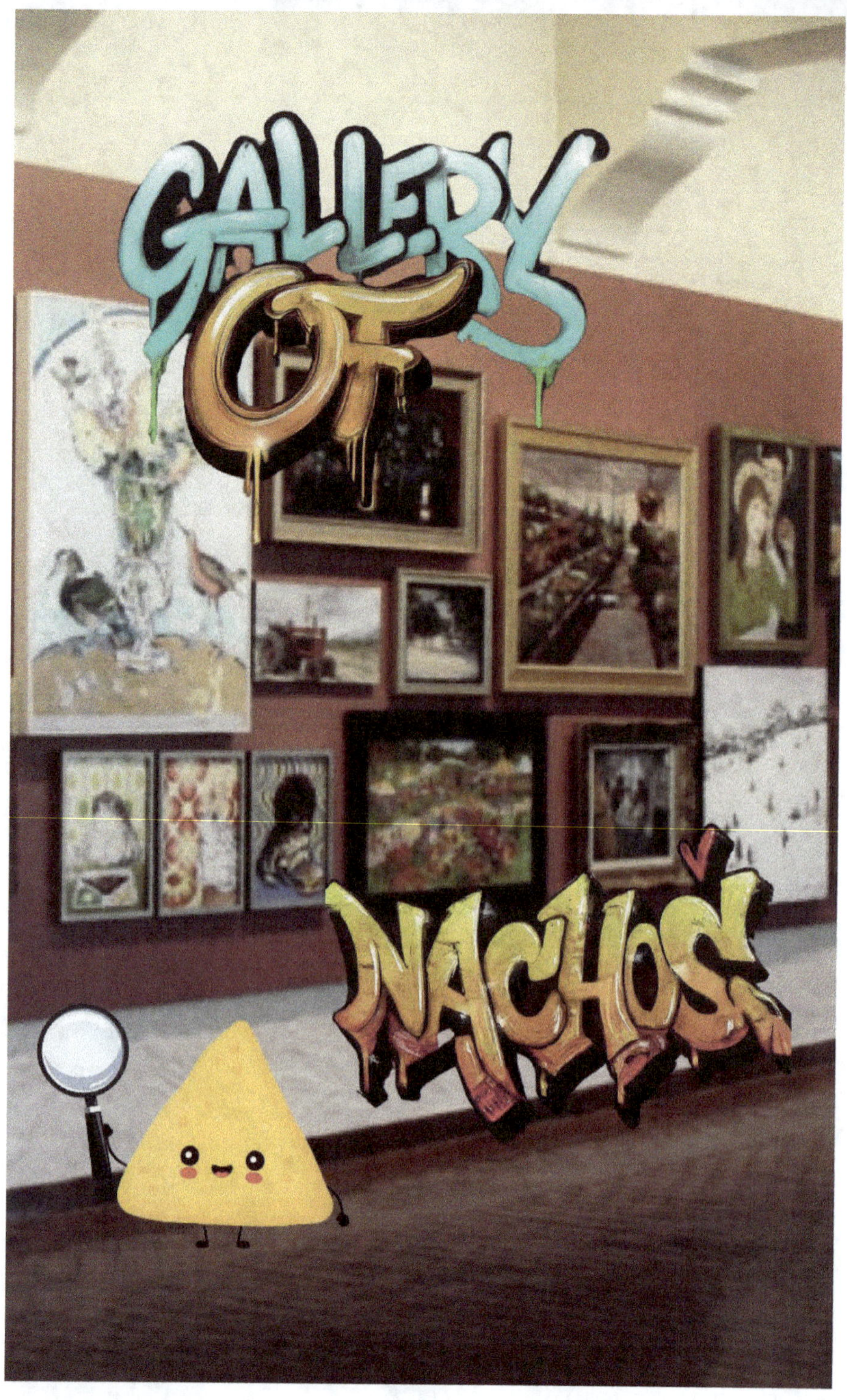
GALLERY OF
NACHOS

GALLERY:

Funny Nacho Art

MICO

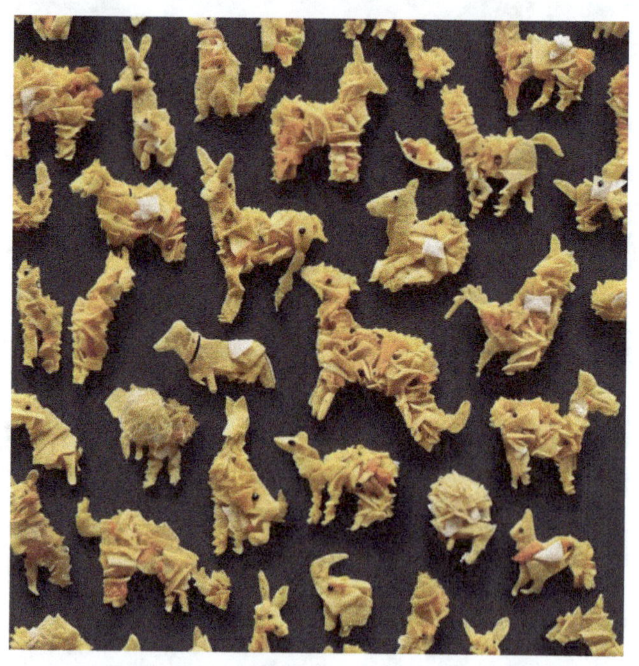

About the Author

The author Brian Hakoun is a passionate wordsmith, wielding the pen like an artist with a brush. With a fervent love for language and storytelling, can he craft narratives that resonate with depth and emotion. Drawing inspiration from the intricacies of everyday life, as well as the profound mysteries of the human experience, his writing

transcends mere words on a page, evoking vivid imagery and stirring the soul. With a keen eye for detail and a heart full of empathy, he explores themes of love, loss, resilience, and the beauty of the human spirit. Through his work, he invites readers on a journey of self-discovery and introspection, leaving an indelible mark on their hearts and minds.

FOX HOLE
PUBLISHING